*The Power of You Series*

# Yes- YOU Matter, YOU Are Enough

by
KARIN J. LUND

Illustrated by Gillian Seaman

*Yes-YOU Matter, YOU Are Enough*

ISBN (Book): 978-1-949955-11-8
ISBN (eBook): 978-1-949955-12-5

For permission requests, contact the author at:
KJLund@G-PowerGlobal.com;
www.g-powerglobalpublishing.com;
www.G-PowerGlobal.com

Illustrations by Gillian Seaman

Printed in the United States of America.

# Dedicated to YOU

YOU

have always been enough.

From
the
moment
YOU
were
born,

YOU
mattered.

YOU
were
enough.

YOU
were
born
from

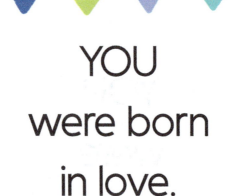

# YOU
## were born
## in love.

# YOU
## were born
## to love.

YOU
were born
knowing how
to sing,
to laugh,
to love,
to smile,
and to dance.

# Yes, dance!

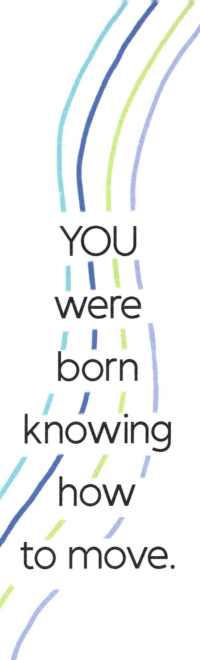

YOU
were
born
knowing
how
to move.

With every
smile, laugh,
giggle, tear,
and every
breath of
your life...

YOU
have
mattered.

YOU
have been
enough.

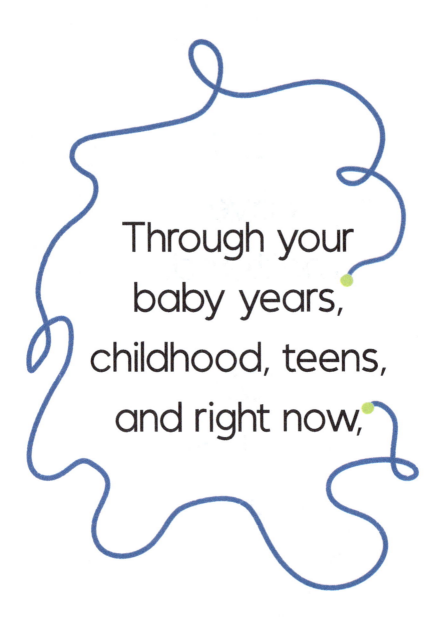

Through your
baby years,
childhood, teens,
and right now,

YOU
have always
mattered.

YOU
have always
been enough.

Along the way,
YOU
might have realized
YOU
could have
been a better
brother/sister,
daughter/son,
student,
cousin, friend,

girlfriend, boyfriend
grandaughter,
or grandson.

Don't worry.

We have all felt this
way at some time.

Just recognizing
this makes
YOU
strive to
be a better person
going forward.

YOU might wish
YOU had a different
relationship with
your parents,
caregivers, or family,
or wish YOU
had spent more
time with them.

Or, hopefully YOU
and your parents,
siblings, caregivers,
family, and friends
get along great.

Just remember,

YOU
matter.

YOU
are
enough.

At a very early age, some people just know what they want to do with their lives.

Some people have a special interest, a gift for playing an instrument, a sport, acting, singing, building, fixing cars, or designing.

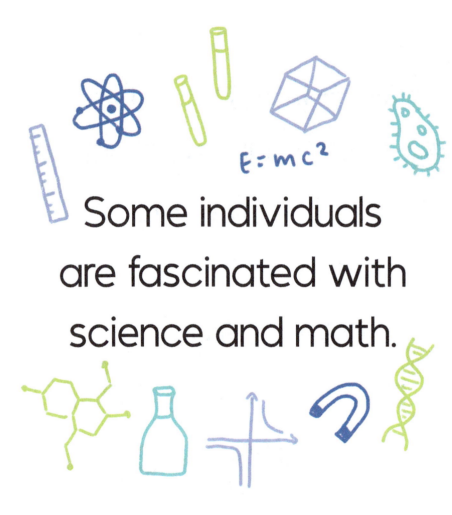

$E = mc^2$

Some individuals
are fascinated with
science and math.

Others are artistic
or prefer to
be outdoors.
Others may want
to design
computer games
or be veterinarians.

Keep noticing what
YOU enjoy and the
skills that come
easily to YOU.

Over time an
interest can become
your passion.

When YOU have a new experience, ask yourself how it makes YOU feel.

Do YOU look forward to repeating that experience?

This is how YOU begin to find your passion.

Over time YOU find
ways to repeat a skill
or activity, or return
to a place that has
meaning for YOU.

YOU may find ways to improve a process, the materials, or equipment YOU need to use for that task.

YOU may watch
videos on YouTube
that show YOU how
to perfect a skill
or task.

YOU
may find
yourself going
somewhere to listen
to someone or
watch someone,
who has pefected
that skill or task.

YOU may find friends or family members, even teachers, who might try to dissuade YOU from pursuing something safe YOU enjoy doing.

Friends may be envious that YOU spend a lot of time practicing and perfecting these skills.

They may be jealous that YOU are naturally talented at something they wish they could do.

They may even try
to encourage YOU
to spend more time
with them rather
than on what
YOU want to do,
or learn,
or perfect.

I believe we are here to discover what we are passionate about.

I've spoken to people who loved doing something when they were younger but never pursued it. When they were older, they regret never having tried.

Don't be
that person!

Oprah says,
"Passion
becomes
purpose."

I say,
"SEEK your passion.
BE your passion.
LIVE your passion."

Find a way to
make passion
and happiness
a relevant part
of your life.

Remember,

YOU
matter.

YOU
are
enough.

Yes,
YOU!

Do YOU feel comfortable with the next step in your life, or are YOU confused about your future?

Many of us are unsure about what we want to do with our lives.

It is OK if YOU are still searching.

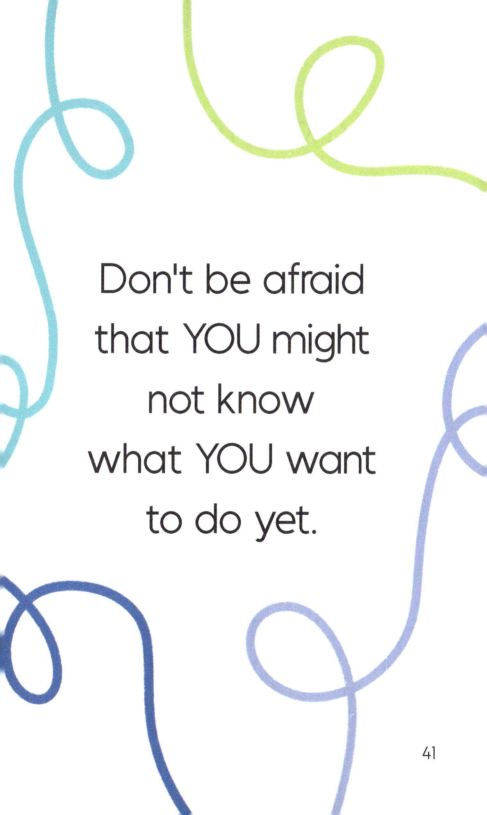

Don't be afraid
that YOU might
not know
what YOU want
to do yet.

In many respects,
we spend the rest
of our lives searching
for understanding,
answers,
and truth.

This is why our
life is called
a "journey."

Yes,
YOU
matter.

YOU
are
enough.

Are YOU comfortable with change or does a shift in plans make YOU uneasy?

Neither reaction is
right or wrong.
The way YOU
respond to change
is just who
YOU are.
And this is OK.

But, how
YOU react
and feel
about change
can impact your life.

If YOU don't like change, YOU might stay in a job, or a relationship that YOU don't like or that isn't helping YOU move toward something that offers more opportunities and happiness.

YOU might shy away
from new places
and experiences
because YOU
are afraid of
change or doing
something different.

Every now and then,
ask yourself,
"Am I not making
a decision, or am I
afraid to make a
decision,
because I am
frightened by
change?"

Even though
we tell ourselves
we don't
mind change,
few of us are
as adaptable
as we think.

Remember,

YOU
matter.

YOU
are
enough.

When something
happens to YOU,
it may not seem
logical, or fair
at the time.

Right now, YOU might be trying to understand how some pieces of your life may not be fitting together very well.

# Write a comment, challenge, or situation on the puzzle pieces on the next two pages.

Is there any commonality that helps YOU shed light on a situation, a challenge, or problem YOU are wrestling with?

Write down what
YOU could change
and how this change
could impact your
life/situation.

Read this statement often.

_____

_____

_____

_____

_____

_____

_____

_____

_____

Remember, change only happens if the process for the change is repeated often over a long period of time.

List small,
incremental steps
YOU envision
helping YOU make
this change happen.
Acknowledge these
small steps
and successes.

YOU may have
to adjust some of
your steps, that's OK.

If YOU need to
backtrack,
that's OK too.

Keep pushing
forward
and celebrate
your succeses
along the way.

# What do I want to change in my life?

What is the step-by-step process YOU are going to implement to make this change happen?

Try to concentrate on one change or challenge at a time.

*NOTE:*
Think about asking someone to be your accountability partner. This person will help reinforce your goals throughout the process and give YOU courage to keep moving forward.

Here we go!

Challenge: _____

_____

_____

_____

_____

Date: _____

Action Item: _____

_____

_____

Status: _____

Date: _____

Action Item: _____

_____

_____

Status: _____

Date: _____

Action Item: _____

_____

_____

Status: _____

Date: _____

Action Item: _____

_____

_____

Status: _____

Date: _____

Action Item: _____

_____

_____

Status: _____

Live from a place where YOU can change how YOU live, reach out, interact with others, connect to your life and the Universe.

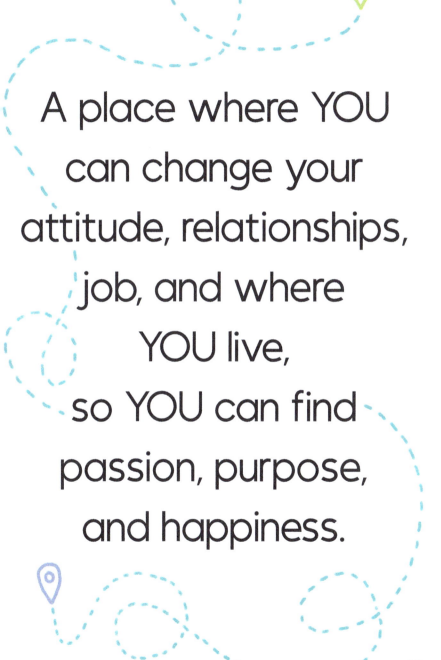

A place where YOU
can change your
attitude, relationships,
job, and where
YOU live,
so YOU can find
passion, purpose,
and happiness.

Because,

YOU
matter.

YOU
are
enough.

Be aware of
how unexpected
meetings, people,
and new places
can lead to
different experiences
and opportunities.

These experiences
may take YOU out
of your comfort zone,
and challenge YOU,
but these
experiences can
also transform
and inspire.

While YOU may not be able to see the future, YOU may be able to feel the Universe pushing YOU in a new direction.

Keep seeking truth
and honesty
in your life.

Don't ever be
afraid to choose
a new path.

Believe YOU can
always decide to
change the direction
of your life
for the better.

Remember,

YOU
matter.

YOU
are
enough.

Sometimes we wish
for something,
and it doesn't
turn out the way
we wanted.

Do YOU blame
yourself, or
someone else
for the results?

Did YOU work
as hard as
YOU could?

Did YOU think
YOU messed up,
misjudged, or
failed?

We need to recognize that an experience or a plan that hasn't turned out the way we thought it should, can be disappointing, but may be life changing.

Disappointments
and even perceived
failures, are part of
our life experiences.
But setbacks are
not the end result,
just part of
the process.

Like learning to
ride a bike.
YOU fall.
YOU pick
yourself up.
YOU try again.
Repeat.

That is what life is.
Lots of experiences
learning how to fall
and pick yourself up,
again, and again,
and again.

Thomas Edison, the inventor of the incandescent lightbulb, among other inventions, once said, "I have not failed 10,000 times, I have successfully found 10,000 ways that did not work."

Oh, by the way,
don't forget to
ask yourself
what YOU learned
from each
experience.

Remember,

YOU
matter.

YOU
are
enough.

Honor and own
your experiences
and choices,
however imperfect
they seem
to YOU.

They brought YOU
to where YOU
are right now.

# Questions???

What have YOU attempted to accomplish or create lately?

Were YOU successful or could the experience have turned out better? Why? Be specific.

_____

_____

_____

_____

_____

_____

_____

_____

_____

_____

Every experience
helps YOU create
a new reality
in your life's
journey,
a new truth.

Because,

YOU

matter.

YOU

are

enough.

The Universe will acknowledge YOU in extraordinary and unique ways when YOU do something good without expecting anything in return.

So, YOU see the
Universe is working
for YOU if YOU
are paying attention.
It will recognize your
kindess, generosity,
and unselfishness.

When something happens to YOU that YOU perceive is bad, the Universe is not punishing YOU.
It is nudging YOU to follow a different direction or make a different choice.

Or, there may be something YOU need to learn or someone YOU need to meet along the way.

Sometimes, something that happens to YOU takes time to understand.

It might be months
or even years
until YOU see
something YOU
might have thought
was not the
outcome YOU had
wanted, turn out
to be positive
in the end.

These experiences
might have guided
YOU toward

a new awareness,
a new experience,
a new person,
a deeper
understanding,
or truth.

Everything that
happens to YOU
contains a
message
and a lesson
if YOU
learn to
listen.

Remember,

YOU
matter.

YOU
are
enough.

When YOU reach within and start to acknowledge your strengths and feelings, YOU discover and reinforce who YOU are and begin to understand why YOU are here.

How does it make
YOU feel when
YOU reach out to
help someone?
Even if it is just
to say, "Good
morning" or "Hi."

Don't YOU feel
good inside?

What if
YOU decide
to reach out to
one person
every day?

YOU might call or
text a friend to ask
how they are.
YOU might help
a sibling, a coworker,
or a friend, with
something they are
struggling with.

YOU might hold a door open for someone or help them carry groceries to a safe place.

YOU could wish a friend "Happy Birthday" or let them know YOU are thinking of them.

YOU could volunteer for a community project, or help build a house for a veteran or family in need.

Sometimes I ask
the Universe
to give me
a way to help
someone that day.

Every time I do this,
I am presented
with an opportunity
to help someone.

Any time YOU feel sorry for yourself, reach out and help someone else instead.

You will immediately feel better.

# See how YOU make the world a better place just by being YOU!

add your picture here

We are meant to
reach out to
one another in
friendship, respect,
love, compassion,
and without hate,
judgement, jealousy,
or envy.

We are meant to
reach out and to
care for and
about each other.

We are meant to live a life knowing that we are valued, but first we must learn to love, respect, and value ourselves.

If we don't love,
respect, and value
ourselves, how do
we teach others to
love, respect
and value us?

Remember,

YOU
matter.

YOU
are
enough.

# YOU see my friend, YOU are the hero of your life.

Draw a picture of a hero YOU want to emulate and add your characteristics. Include your hair color, style, and anything else that makes YOU, YOU!

YOU control your
feelings
and thoughts.
↓ ↓ ↓
YOU are your own
cheerleader and
champion.

Yes, YOU!

Don't blame your
life on someone else
because YOU don't
want to take
responsibility for
your choices.

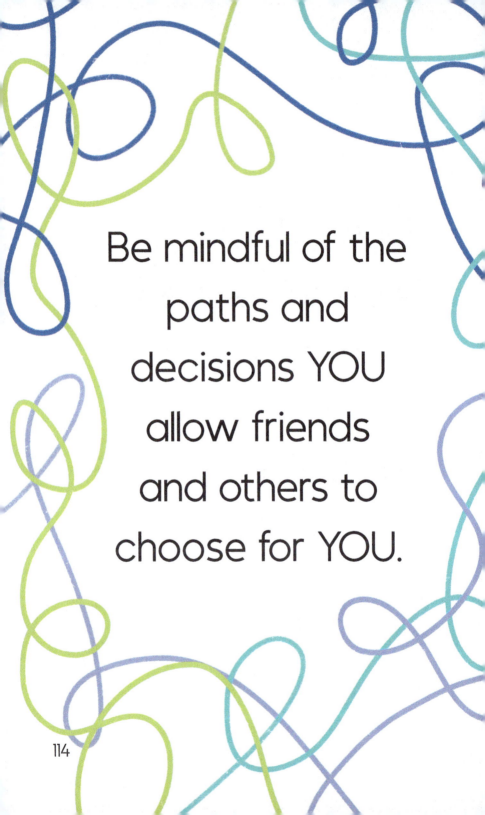

Be mindful of the paths and decisions YOU allow friends and others to choose for YOU.

Don't give your power away by asking someone else to make decisions for YOU.

(Then blame them when a choice or decision doesn't go the way YOU think it should.)

Instead, find people who challenge your thoughts, decisions, and opinions about yourself, and the world around YOU in a good, positive way.

Have YOU ever watched
*The Wizard of Oz?*

It is a remarkable film about a young girl, who has a life-changing adventure because of a devastating tornado.

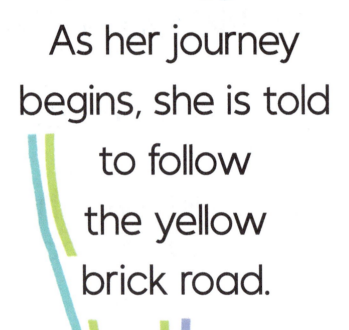

As her journey begins, she is told to follow the yellow brick road.

The story is about
who she
encounters on her
way to meet
the great
Wizard of Oz
at the end of the
yellow brick road.

Look for special people on your yellow brick road. They are guides for YOU in this life.

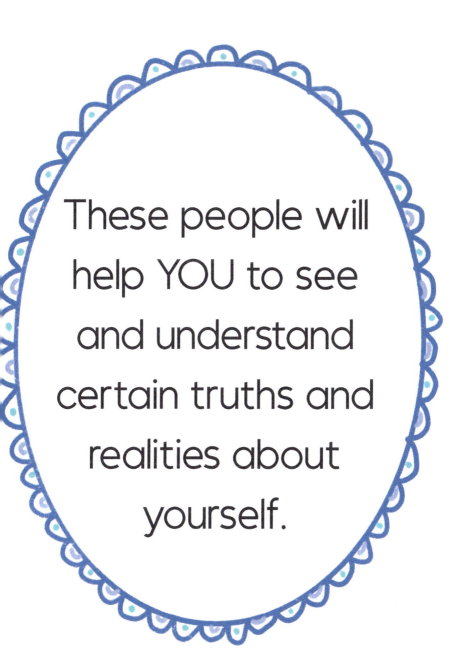

These people will help YOU to see and understand certain truths and realities about yourself.

They may challenge YOU to think about how YOU look at your life and help guide YOU, if YOU take the time to listen.

Remember,

YOU
matter.

YOU
are
enough.

Keep asking
yourself
what feels
right for YOU.

Don't allow
anyone to make
YOU feel guilty
for saying
"NO."

Imagine someone asking YOU a question YOU don't want to answer or asking YOU to go someplace or do something YOU don't want to do.

Practice saying
"NO" out loud.
Look in the mirror
and watch and
listen to yourself
say "NO."

Be ready for a
guilt trip or
backlash from a
so-called friend,
boyfriend, partner,
or co-worker,
when YOU say "NO."

There almost
always
is some kind of
backlash or
particularly hurtful
words.

A partner
may threaten to
break up with YOU.
A friend may bully
YOU on social media.
But stay strong.

# "NO" means "No."

Don't back down
because of the
backlash or
hurtful words,
even though it might
be hard for YOU.

# Do YOU remember a time when YOU stood up for yourself?

## How did it make YOU feel?

_____

_____

_____

_____

_____

_____

_____

_____

_____

Remember to
tell yourself,
"I am learning to
love the sound of
my feet walking
away from things
not meant for me."
AG

This means
saying "NO" too.

Because,

YOU
matter.

YOU
are
enough.

Did YOU ever have a friend, or a person who magically seemed to come into your life right when YOU needed them?

Oftentimes, people will be placed directly in your path because YOU need to learn something from them.

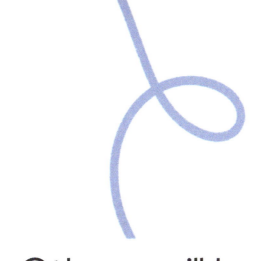

Others will have
a much quieter
impact. These are
who I call the
"Whisperers."

Their messages
are more subtle,
but the lessons they
impart are
sometimes what
YOU need to
learn the most.

Listen for the
"Whisperers"
in your life.

— — — — — — — —

The "Whisperers"
in your life may
be people of
action and
not words.

Are your friends supportive and do they help make YOU a better person?

Are your friends motivated to make themselves and the world a better place?

Are they compassionate and careful about how they treat others?

Do they reach out
within the
community to
help someone else?

Sometimes, we have friends who encourage us to be less than we are capable of being.

Do YOU have someone like this in your life?

As I mentioned earlier, sometimes friends bully YOU on social media and make YOU feel bad about yourself.

These are not friends.

Don't be afraid to
let go of people
in your life who
are toxic
and negative.

Although, it is
hard to walk away
from someone
YOU thought was
a friend.
Sometimes it is
just what YOU
need to do.

Remember,
some people
are only meant
to be in your
life for a
short time.

So, don't be
afraid to,

Let them go.

Let them go.

Let them go.

Let them go.

Instead, surround yourself with people who are positive, who make YOU feel good about yourself and who support YOU, and care about YOU.

Negativity creates more negativity.

Positivity creates more positivity.

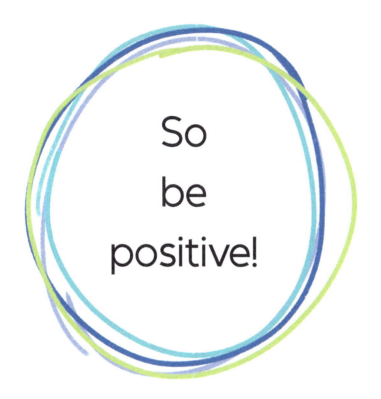

So
be
positive!

Remember,

YOU
matter.

YOU
are
enough.

Yes, YOU.

Don't take people
for granted.

They are not here
to serve YOU.

Nurture your
positive friendships,
even if they are
short-lived.

YOU never know when YOU might need to work with a previous friend or need their wisdom and advice again in your life.

Treasure the
people who choose
to stand beside
YOU through
all the ups and
downs in
your life.

They are
true gifts.

They accept
YOU for
who YOU are.

Remember,

YOU
matter.

YOU
are
enough.

# What is your definition of a friend?

_____

_____

_____

_____

_____

_____

_____

_____

_____

_____

# How do YOU reach out as a friend?

Do YOU wait for friends to contact YOU all the time or do YOU reach out to them?

_____

_____

_____

_____

_____

_____

_____

_____

_____

# What is your definition of health?

## What are YOU doing to stay healthy?

_____

_____

_____

_____

_____

_____

_____

_____

_____

# What is your definition of a relationship?

What do YOU want your partner or friend to be like?

_____

_____

_____

_____

_____

_____

_____

_____

_____

_____

Remember,

YOU
matter.

YOU
are
enough.

Yes, YOU.

Many people think that money equals happiness or that success is measured by the car YOU drive, where YOU live, the clothes YOU wear, or how much money YOU make.

It is OK to want those things. Just don't get caught up in thinking that owning "things" is who YOU are inside.

YOU also need to ask yourself what YOU are willing to do, become, or give up, to own these things or have a certain lifestyle.

No amount of
money is worth
losing the good,
healthy relationships
YOU have with
your friends, family,
and co-workers.

# What is your definition of success?

_____

_____

_____

_____

_____

_____

_____

_____

_____

_____

If YOU can acquire
all of the things
YOU listed, and your
social life, work life,
dating life, or family
life is strong and
YOU have surrounded
yourself with

people who have
good, positive
values that YOU
respect, then
YOU are building
inward success.
This is not
easy to do, but
GREAT JOB!

Or, have YOU surrounded yourself with people who are constantly comparing what they have to everyone else? Are YOU this way too?

This is not
→ inward success. ←
This is what some
refer to as
← outward success. →

Outward success
does not
guarantee
happiness.

It is caring and
reaching out to
help one another
that counts.
It is leading with
compassion and
empathy that
matters.

Ask yourself what your commitment is toward making the world a better place.

# Circle your answers:

Are YOU a great friend,
partner, spouse, sibling,
or son/daughter?

Yes   No

Are YOU reliable as a
friend or employee?

Yes   No

Do YOU support and
promote your friends,
siblings, or partners?

Yes   No

Do YOU help with
community projects such
as Habitat for Humanity
or Big Brothers/Big Sisters?

Yes  No

Did YOU ever think about
volunteering at a
community center and
helping coach a sports team?

Yes  No

Did YOU ever think about
creating a business or
working in a company that
has a culture that
respects employees?

Yes  No

# Life Chart

# What is important to YOU?

Number the following items from most important (1) to least important (14)

____ Integrity     ____ Success
____ Honesty      ____ Money
____ Trust        ____ Security
____ Health       ____ House, Cars
____ Family       ____ Jewelry
____ Friends      ____ Volunteering
____ Religion     ____ Respect

Let this life chart remind YOU
what is important to YOU.
When YOU feel challenged look at
this chart to help guide YOU.

Don't hesitate to review and make a change on your life chart, but ask yourself "WHY are YOU changing something?"

_____

_____

_____

_____

_____

_____

_____

YOU might even ask yourself why these areas are important to YOU. This is also a good discussion to have with your partner and friends.

Your VALUES will
be challenged
during your lifetime.

Your GOALS will be
diverted, questioned,
or even ridiculed
over the course
of your life.

Your CHOICES will
be undermined
during your life.

Remember,
all actions
have
consequences.

Accept responsibility for your choices.

Accept responsibility for your decisions.

Just because YOU say YOU are "sorry" doesn't mean YOU will be forgiven.

YOU are not
owed a second
chance, even if
YOU think YOU
deserve it.

Sometimes saying
"I am sorry"
will never be enough.

However difficult,
this too,
will be a life lesson.

This is your path,
your journey,
your jog down the
yellow brick road.

Be proud of your
accomplishments.

Let them make
YOU smile
and shine.

Too many times we
only remember
what we don't
do well, or what
we struggle with.

Make a list of
your gifts,
accomplishments,
and all the positive
comments that
people have
mentioned to YOU.

Keep this list
updated so YOU
have a place
YOU can go
to remind YOU of
who YOU are.

# My Special Skills & Talents

# My Special Skills & Talents

# My Special Skills & Talents

Because,

YOU
matter.

YOU
are
enough.

Yes, YOU!

Take the hits as they come, and they will come.

Learn to accept and take responsibility for the decisions YOU have made and try not to repeat the mistakes.

But realize, YOU
will repeat some
of your mistakes
until YOU understand
what is behind
making
those same
mistakes time
and time again.

It might be fear,
insecurity, or
uncertainty.
Take a leap of
faith here.
Ask for help to
keep moving forward
and envision a new
future for yourself.

Our lives have mattered more because of YOU being here.

Wow, did YOU
ever think of this?
Our lives
are better
because of YOU.
YES, YOU!

Thank YOU for recognizing that our lives have always mattered too.

Remember,

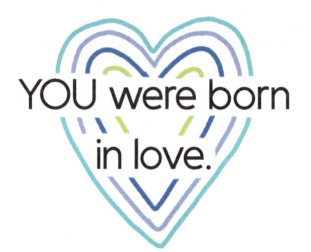

YOU were born
in love.

YOU were born
from love.

YOU

were

born

to

YOU were born
knowing how
to sing,
to laugh,
to smile,
to dance,
YES, dance!

YOU were born
knowing that
your life
matters
and that
YOU
are
enough.

Today, reach
out to someone
YOU care about
and tell them
why YOU think
they are special –
and thank them.

The Universe is always ready to share its beauty, and abundance with YOU.

The Universe is
prepared to
teach YOU and
help YOU
recognize something
or someone
that YOU need
to meet and know.

THANK YOU!

Just keep
watching
and remember
to say,
"thank YOU"
and acknowledge
this gift.

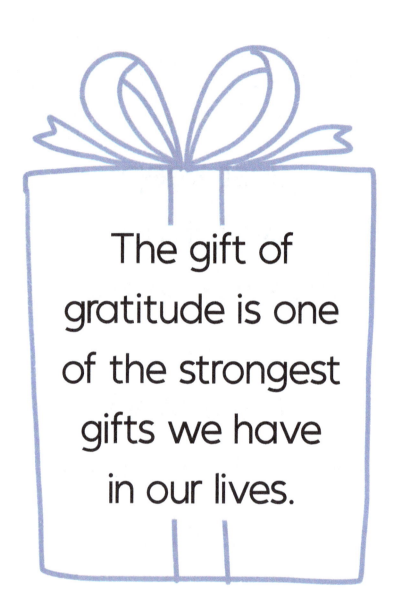

The gift of gratitude is one of the strongest gifts we have in our lives.

Thank the Universe for a beautiful day.

Thank the
Universe for an
idea that
magically appears
in your thoughts
or as a
solution to a
challenge.

Thank the Universe for helping YOU to see a clear path toward a career, a life decision, or guiding YOU toward something YOU love to do.

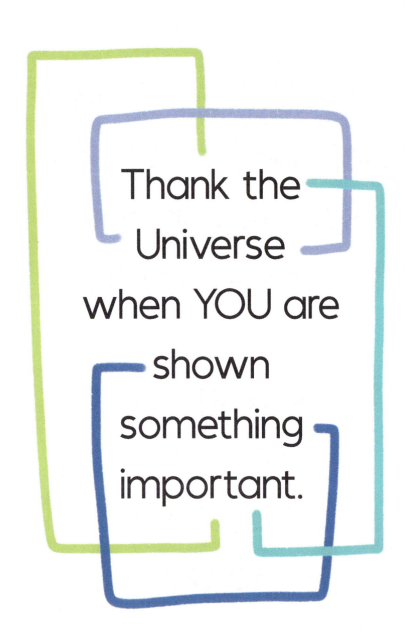

Thank the Universe when YOU are shown something important.

End each day
saying
"thank YOU"
for the gifts
from the day.

Because,

YOU
matter.

YOU
are
enough.

Thank YOU
for being born.
Thank YOU
for sharing this
beautiful, messy,
sometimes hard,
wonderful life
with us.

Many people have
been privileged to
be on this journey
with YOU.

YOU will welcome
many more people
into your life as
YOU go forward
on your journey.

Thank YOU
for showing
us how
different
journeys
can be
travelled.

Look at yourself
in the mirror
and every
day say,
MY LIFE MATTERS!
I MATTER!
I AM ENOUGH!

Remember to
tell yourself,
"I am
PERFECT
as I am."

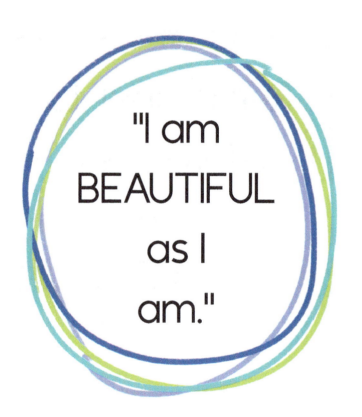

"I am BEAUTIFUL as I am."

Keep learning.
Keep seeing.
Keep feeling.
Keep reaching out.

Keep your heart
open to love,
wonder,
and the magic
of surprise.

YOU are a
beautiful spirit
with a
beautiful mind.

Be good
to yourself.

Yours is a unique
journey because
it is YOUR
journey.

Never forget YOU
are the star of
your own life.

YOU are your
own hero
for YOU.

YOU are never a
victim in your life
if YOU don't allow
yourself to feel
like YOU are
a victim.

The world is already a better place because YOU are in it.

Let's share our love and gratitude for this life, however challenging.

# Remember,

## I matter.
## I am enough.
## I celebrate ME today.

add
your
photo
here!

My life has always mattered.

I have always mattered.

# Celebrate
# YOU
# today,
# tomorrow,
# and
# forever.

Because,

Yes–
I matter,
I am
enough.

# Thoughts I want to add...

_____

_____

_____

_____

_____

_____

_____

_____

_____

_____

_____

_____

# A note from Karin...

I've come to understand that the message in this book is both deeply personal and widely relatable. At some point, we all grapple with questions about our relevance, whether within our families, among friends, in teams, organizations, or the workplace.

There are times when we find ourselves as the sole voice of dissent in a discussion, meeting, relationship, or conference. In those moments, it's essential to OWN our voice, our thoughts, and our right to be present. Your perspective matters, even when others disagree.

This book serves as a powerful reminder of our uniqueness, our worth, and the truth that we are enough just as we are. It encourages readers to take full ownership of their decisions rather than handing that power over to someone else. It calls us to look inward for the strength and conviction to reaffirm our value.

We must recognize our strengths and accept our weaknesses because doing so helps us stay resilient, true to ourselves and receptive to these areas in others.

When we strengthen our inner resolve, we naturally fortify our outward presence. By taking responsibility for our thoughts and actions, we build the confidence to stand in any room, look anyone in the eye, and say with certainty:

**My opinion matters.**
**My thoughts matter.**
**I am enough.**

No one can take that truth away from you, no one. Lead with compassion, respect, and kindness, and always remember:

**Yes–**
**I matter.**
**I am enough.**

# Acknowledgements

Thank you to Sid and Haley for serving as teen advisors/consultants for this book. Their comments and thoughts were invaluable and added greatly to the content and message that the author wanted to convey.

Thank you Gillian for your creative expertise, illustrations, thoughts and advice. You have been instrumental in the publishing of this book.

To everyone who shared their comments, ideas, inspiration and editing for this book, I can't thank you enough.

# Additional Books by Karin J. Lund

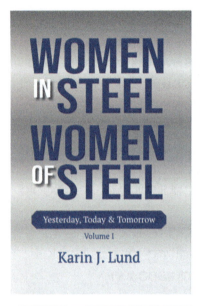

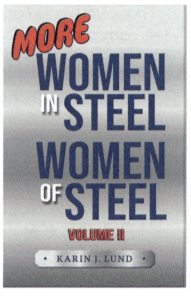

# STEAM Rising

## Tech & Trades
### Build. Think. Lead.

STEAM Rising is a dynamic program designed to inspire 8th-12th grade girls to explore, grow, and thrive in STEM and STEAM fields.

Rooted in the belief that communication, wellness, and resilience are just as vital as technical skills, the program empowers young women to recognize their strengths and embrace their potential.

Through inspiring stories of trailblazing women, engaging discussions with engineers and trades professionals, and practical guidance on building networks and leadership skills, STEAM Rising helps students see what's possible for their futures.

With a focus on confidence, self-worth, and opportunity, it encourages every young woman to say with conviction: I matter. I am enough.

If you would like to participate in this program or become a corporate or personal sponsor, contact Karin Lund at KJLund@G-PowerGlobal.com.